Table (

THE ELEVENTH HOUR SERVANTS

JAMES BROWN

The Eleventh Hour Servants
By James Brown
Word Of Grace International Ministries
First Edition - Copyright 1998
Printed in the USA by WP Publishing
www.workinperkins.com

Introduction

Introduction

etween 1970 and 1973, I was the co-founder, president, and overseer for a youth ministry in a small rural community in southeast Colorado. During that time the Lord gave me a vivid and powerful night vision or dream. In the dream I was in the ocean sitting on a surfboard waiting for a good wave to ride to shore. As I waited, I noticed that it was a very calm and peaceful day. The water was just right, and I sensed an excitement about "catching the next wave." Suddenly I sensed a swell moving under my surfboard that started to nudge me forward. When this happened, I actually felt a tangible anointing of the Holy Spirit pulsate through my entire being. However, I did not catch the wave in time, and it went to shore without me. Again, this same thing happened, but this time the swell, the anointing, and the presence of God grew much stronger. It was an awesome feeling that surged through my whole being, however, for some reason, I was not able to fully catch this wave and it rolled under my surfboard rushing to shore, and leaving me behind.

As I sat on my surfboard waiting for the next wave, I began to realize the next wave would be much larger than the previous waves, which caused me great concern, because I knew my surfing skills were scarcely sufficient to handle three to four feet waves (years prior to this dream, while stationed in Hawaii, I actually tried surfing on small waves). I began to sense the wave rolling in, and said to myself, "I can't surf that well, but if I don't catch this wave it will crush me." So with fear and trembling, I lay on my board and began to paddle with the movement of the swelling surf, knowing I had to catch this enormous wave. I lay there paddling rapidly on my surfboard, and then slowly stood up shaking and trembling. Immediately this swell peaked into a massive wall of surf that thrust me upward and forward, propelling me to an unimaginable ride, one that was both thrilling and frightening. The wave began to rise beneath me, as it moved me toward shore. While this happened, I could feel the most awesome and tangible presence of God I have ever experienced in my life. This mountain of surf literally shot me to shore with tremendous speed and power. It was in control, as I simply yielded to its force. This unimaginable experience and exhilarating ride left me nearly breathless, almost as though I had been shot out of a cannon.

When I arrived on the shore, I saw what seemed to be broken bottles, debris, and barbed wire fencing. The landscape looked like a war zone. It was quite depressing, especially after such a glorious and wonderful ride. As I surveyed the scene, from a location just above the ground, I noticed that the sky was very dark and ominous. Next, I heard myself saying, "How are we ever going to get over all of this?" When I said this—suddenly I was awakened.

The Lord confirmed the dream through a series of events, and as I sought the Lord I began to realize that He was showing me things about my spiritual journey with Him, and things that would transpire in the last day Church.

May this book serve to sound a prophetic trumpet in your spirit. End-time events are falling into place more rapidly than many realize, and we are living in the season of final harvest. Divine destiny is being fulfilled at an alarming pace, and the momentum is being accelerated in both the camp of God and the camp of the enemy.

Yet while this is happening, many of us, who are educated in the Word of God and blessed to our toes, have failed to become actively involved in winning men and women, boys and girls for Jesus Christ. This must and will change in this upcoming move of the Holy Spirit.

There is no time to idly sit on the sidelines and merely watch these events unfold. God has not called you and me to be spectators. To become doers of God's Word, we must get healed and strengthened, so we can reach the lost and fulfill our part in the increase of God's Kingdom, while edifying the church of Jesus Christ.

It is important to realize that while the Holy Spirit is stirring the Body of Christ (especially in North America) to awaken and repent of its current condition of apathy and worldliness, the adversary is seeking to "wear out the saints." He seeks to "steal, kill and destroy" anyone and everyone that is not born again or walking according to the Word of God. There is always a simultaneous activity going on in the world when it comes to spiritual matters. Nothing is static in the spirit realm. God is moving, and the enemy is moving.

The Eleventh Hour Servants

A prominent prophetic voice in this hour said, "By the end, everyone will either be God possessed or devil possessed." I think he must be correct. The middle of the road position is narrowing each day (though there has never really been a middle of the road with God).

Whose side will you be on? The Apostle Paul warned believers to examine themselves and to make sure they were in the faith (2 Corinthians 13:5) and not reprobates. Certainly, this admonition is applicable for us today. None of us are exempt from the wiles of the enemy, or the weaknesses of the flesh.

I pray that this book will be a tool to minister to readers who know they have not fulfilled the purpose and call of God upon their lives. May the Holy Spirit use it to bring you a fresh zeal, courage, and inspiration to "run the race" set before you. As you read these pages may you too hear the Father saying, "It is time for you to become My—*Eleventh Hour Servants*"

James Brown

What Is an Eleventh Hour Servant?

O ne of the most exciting things you and I will be privileged to partake in is the end-time harvest of souls. This is a major event that will supersede anything we have seen thus far. Even now there are great mass crusades taking place throughout the world with renowned ministries such as that of Morris Cerullo, Reinhard Bonnke, Benny Hinn, and many others. These individual ministries have witnessed tens of thousands, and even hundreds of thousands coming to receive Christ in one service or crusade. As phenomenal as that is, we have yet to see and experience the move of God during the time of the Eleventh Hour Servants.

The question we might ask is, "What is an Eleventh Hour Servant?" Answering this question will help us to find out where we are in the scheme of things with regards to the fulfillment of God's promise to fill the earth with the gospel of Jesus Christ (Matthew 24:14). If we are not already in the fields and reaping the harvest, we definitely want to be in this final group of soul winners and be prepared for the return of our Lord.

The Eleventh Hour Servants

Simply stated, Eleventh Hour Servants are going to be a group of believers that will arise and take their place in the harvest fields right next to those who have labored and borne the heat of the day during the first ten hours and fifty-nine minutes of the harvest. They are going to be the "final remnant" that Jesus will send out to the fields. In fact, their arrival in the fields will be a signal that we are nearly at the close of the day, yet they will have a key role in completing the harvest work before the sun goes down on this final generation.

What Jesus Said about the Eleventh Hour Servants

I t seems obvious that we are living in the last of the last days, as most theologians and Bible scholars will agree. The passage of scripture this book springs from deals with the last day and hour before Jesus returns. It is found in Matthew 20:1-16. Let's examine it before we proceed.

1. *For the kingdom of heaven is like unto a man that is an householder, which went out early in the morning to hire labourers into his vineyard.*

2. *And when he had agreed with the labourers for a penny a day, he sent them into his vineyard.*

3. *And he went out about the third hour, and saw others standing idle in the marketplace,*

4. *And said unto them; Go ye also into the vineyard, and whatsoever is right I will give you. And they went their way.*

5. *Again he went out about the sixth and ninth hour, and did likewise.*

6. *And about the eleventh hour he went out, and found others standing idle, and saith unto them, Why stand ye here all the day idle?*

7. *They say unto him, Because no man hath hired us. He saith unto them, Go ye also into the vineyard; and whatsoever is right, that shall ye receive.*

8. *So when even was come, the lord of the vineyard saith unto his steward, Call the labourers, and give them their hire, beginning from the last unto the first.*

9. *And when they came that were hired about the eleventh hour, they received every man a penny.*

10. *But when the first came, they supposed that they should have received more; and they likewise received every man a penny.*

11. *And when they had received it, they murmured against the goodman of the house,*

12. *Saying, These last have wrought but one hour, and thou hast made them equal unto us, which have borne the burden and heat of the day.*

13. *But he answered one of them, and said, Friend, I do thee no wrong: didst not thou agree with me for a penny?*

14. *Take that thine is, and go thy way: I will give unto this last, even as unto thee.*

15. *Is it not lawful for me to do what I will with mine own? Is thine eye evil, because I am good?*

16. *So the last shall be first, and the first last: for many be called, but few chosen.*

MATTHEW 20:1-16

It is clear that this parable was not a discourse on church meetings. Jesus was talking about a householder, his vineyard, his harvest, and his readiness to pay laborers for harvesting his crops.

When we look at this parable of the Eleventh Hour Servants, we notice several things.

1. The Eleventh Hour Servants were as physically capable laborers as those already working in the fields.

2. They were not actively working during the beginning of the harvest.

3. They seemingly had the same understanding and skills necessary to harvest as those that had arrived in the fields earlier.

4. They seemed to be hindered from arriving at the marketplace earlier in the day when most laborers gathered and waited to be hired.

5. The lord of the vineyard placed no difference between them and the others that were already working in his fields.

6. They were hired and immediately sent to the fields to work.

7. They were paid for their labor.

Chapter Three

Characteristics of Eleventh Hour Servants?

Have you ever wondered why some people seem to succeed in life, while others are passed by and never seem to arise to their full potential? It may have something to do with chance, but usually has more to do with preparation coming into alignment with an opportunity. The Eleventh Hour Servants are going to be a group of believers that have been waiting on the sidelines for an opportunity, but they will also be prepared by God to do the work. Here is a partial list of some of the characteristics of the Eleventh Hour Servants and how they will play a major role in the end-time harvest.

1. They will be grateful for the opportunity to work.

You see, these servants somehow missed the opportunity to put in a full days work, but now the Lord of the vineyard will be calling them out and rushing them to the fields to glean His harvest.

2. They will be fresh and able to work right alongside the best of the other workers who started early in the day.

Although they are late on the scene, they will not be falling behind in the work they have agreed to do for the Lord of the vineyard.

3. They will be mindful of the wages that await them.

Unlike some laborers who start well and then get disgruntled with their boss and their job situation, these employees will be rejoicing that they have a job that will afford them wages commensurate with that of the rest of the crew.

4. They will be focused.

After hearing the urgency in the voice of the owner of the vineyard, and the lateness of the day, these servants will be fully focused on completing the task of reaping the harvest.

5. They will be happy to be a part of the great end-time harvest of souls.

Because it appears these servants nearly missed working in the harvest, they will most likely be among the happiest laborers in the field, rejoicing that the Lord has offered them such a wonderful opportunity to co-labor with Him.

6. They will not be ashamed that they are arriving in the fields at the last hour.

These laborers will not be plagued with concern or insecurities over those that have started before them or their accomplishments. They will not be distracted or concerned how the other workers perceive them. And, they will not be driven with a sense of unworthiness, but only a sense of purpose.

7. They will finish their course with joy.

These last shall be first and shall rejoice to see the end of the harvest and their work rewarded.

There are also other characteristics of the Eleventh Hour Servants that I want to mention. These characteristics no doubt had to be a part of the other servants already in the field.

I believe the Eleventh Hour Servants will be given to prayer and fasting. They will be individuals who are committed to fervent prayer, and who will realize the need to push away from even the legitimate natural things of life that so easily distract and desensitize us to the things of God.

These end-time servants will have to be free from the sin of sedition, a sin which causes other believers to back off from their commitment to the spiritual authority God has placed them under. They will have to guard their hearts and minds and keep their lips from speaking evil against God's other anointed servants. This does not mean they can never deal with serious issues in a godly way or correct a brother or sister in love and humility. It does mean that they will not be guilty of the destructive gossip and slander that has characterized so much of the church world today.

They will be mindful of the great commission and the obligation of the hour, and having counted the cost, they will disregard all options for the easy way out. I believe many of these individuals will be the so-called rejects or misfits of society. Most of us would question their potential to be useful. But, in the last hour, Jesus will be calling them and sending them to work with the most "elite" workers in the field.

Many will be from broken homes and marriages, and some may be impoverished or uneducated, but the Lord will make room for them right alongside His finest servants.

Among those in this group of Eleventh Hour Servants will be an army of youth that have been overlooked in many churches, and others yet to turn to the Lord. These seemingly unqualified and previously ignored servants will be anointed, appointed and sent out to the harvest. They too will harvest along with the "best of the best."

In fact, one of our daughters was involved in a program for teens that has a radical approach to reaching and revolutionizing young people for Christ. This program is among the best that I have seen thus far. The emphasis of this group is to take troubled teens and turn them into spiritual titans for the Lord. There have been dramatic and marvelous testimonies of young people turning away from drugs, homosexuality and lesbianism, violence, crime, alcoholism, rape, incest, and about everything you can imagine. God is taking these teenagers and totally transforming their lives through His Word and by His Spirit.

They are being equipped to take His Word to the streets, churches, and schools across America. These teens are turning away from Rock, Hip Hop, and Rap music, and are now learning to honor God through sincere worship and praise. These are the type of Eleventh Hour Servants God is developing in this hour. Something powerful is beginning to happen in the world through the youth God is raising up, and I fully expect them to abruptly erupt onto the scene and impact the masses with the Good News. Yes, the Church is slowly but surely on the rise, and the gates of hell shall not prevail against it.

Can God Use Me?

Some who are reading this book have longed to be used mightily by God. You have prayed, fasted, had hands placed upon you by anointed men and women of God, read books, gone to conventions, and studied for hours, but you have not obeyed the call. God sees your hunger and knows what has held you back, but today He is saying, "Enough is enough! Go into My fields and reap, and you will receive My reward."

Even though you may have wasted years in self-pity, fear, unbelief, or some besetting sin, God is now exhorting you to arise, cleanup, and be counted.

He wants you to repent, so He can use you. You can be His mouth piece. You can turn many to Jesus Christ. Your life is not over my friend. The grace, power, and anointing of God is sufficient for you.

So many people in the Body have been broken with heavy trials, burdens, stress, depression, rejection, fear, guilt, and condemnation; they cannot even hold their heads up to the Lord. But God is saying, *"...make straight paths for your feet, so that what is lame may not be dislocated, but rather be healed"* (Hebrews 12:13).

There are those reading this book whose hearts are broken because of some "failure." They feel they are disqualified from serving the Lord in any meaningful capacity. Let me tell you, there is no reason to believe that, especially when we read the scripture.

Look at Moses who killed an Egyptian or David who killed an innocent man and took his wife. How about Peter who denied the Lord three times with cursing or the prodigal son who squandered all of his inheritance? Let's not forget the woman at the well whose testimony brought the whole town to Jesus, or Mary Magdalene who had seven devils cast out of her (and yet, was the first to see Jesus after His resurrection). On and on we can go. These were all people of like passions as all of us, but they yielded their lives to God and were used mightily to fulfill His purpose in the hour in which they lived.

The only thing that can really hold you back from doing the will of God is you and a faulty belief system that says, "You are inferior, too unqualified, or the worst member in the Body of Christ, and there is no way God can use you." Satan wants you to believe that the grace and mercy of God cannot reach your situation. He may even move upon well meaning Christian brothers and sisters to point a legalistic finger of condemnation at you, but remember what the Apostle Paul said through the inspiration and guidance of the Holy Spirit:

> *Who are you to judge another's servant? To his own master he stands or falls. Indeed, he will be made to stand, for God is able to make him stand.*
>
> ROMANS 14:4 NKJV

Look at Proverbs 24:16.

> *For a righteous man may fall seven times and rise again, but the wicked shall fall by calamity (NKJV- emphasis added).*

It is apparent that God has the last say as to when the round and fight is over. I can almost hear Him saying, "The fight has just begun devil, and My Blood-bought, redeemed men and women will rise up and tread you under feet, through My Word and power!" Hallelujah!

Yes, I am aware that there has been an outbreak of slander, divorce, adultery, teenage rebellion, fornication, and financial improprieties within the Church during this generation. Sadly, America has suffered tremendous setbacks from this moral epidemic that has even ravaged the Body of Christ. Obviously, the devil knows his time is short and that God is about to visit the earth in an unprecedented fashion, therefore he is trying to destroy homes, marriages, families, and churches in order to thwart the plan of God.

There are consequences for sin and disobedience to God's Word, regardless of what it might be. But, the Word of God also teaches us that Jesus Christ is the propitiation for our sins and that if we confess our sins, God will be *"faithful and just to forgive our sins and to cleanse us FROM ALL UNRIGHTEOUSNESS"* (1 John 1:9, 2:1-2). You must treat the Word of God as the truth and let every man be a liar who decides to argue with God's eternal wisdom. Without question, I am sure the enemy has tried those tricks on millions in the Body of Christ (me included), but I want you to join me now and shout it from the housetops, "It won't work devil! Jesus has the last word. He is the author and finisher of our faith. He said, *I will never leave you nor forsake you.* He that began a good work in us will complete it until the day of Jesus Christ!"

Maybe you think your situation, sin, or failure is too big to overcome. That is a lie from the pit of hell. Again, I must say, there are consequences across the board for our shortcomings, sins, and failures, but we are forgiven when we admit we have sinned, made poor judgments, and disobeyed God's Word. The Heavenly Father patiently waits for us with outstretched arms, longing for us to admit our need of His unmerited favor and grace to restore us and make us whole. Remember the prodigal son? Jesus shared that truth to give His people hope when they fall. He loves you and wants to make you into a new vessel. Will you give Him an opportunity to prove it to you?

After more than thirty years of ministry, I know of no one who has walked perfectly before God all the days of his or her life. Do you? However, we can be hard on ourselves when we blow it and miss the mark. Like Peter, we can say, "I go fishing." In other words, I blew it! I am finished with the ministry or calling of God. I will go back to my "8 to 5" job.

Most likely, some who are reading this book are not in the ministry today or fulfilling your call because you are more concerned with man's opinion, than what Jesus says about you. Sister Loose Lips has said, "Why should he or she preach or prophesy? They did this or that." Not realizing they are being like the Pharisee who said in his prayer time, *"God. I thank You that I am not like other men—extortioners, unjust, adulterers, or even as this tax collector"* (who was quietly praying next to him Luke 18:11, NKJV).

I remember a story Kenneth Hagin shared concerning an incident that occurred while he was pastor of a small church. He said that during a particular service someone in the congregation gave forth a message in tongues. Following the tongue, a woman (who was not considered very spiritual by some), got up and interpreted the message. Brother Hagin said to the Lord, "Lord I know what this person did just before coming into the church. Why couldn't You have used sister so and so instead? She is a faithful member who tithes, and is always at every service. It would have been better received if she would have interpreted the message." The Lord quickly rebuked him by saying, "Yes, I know this one who gave the interpretation did something before she came into the church, but she repented and I forgave her. This other woman, however, that you wanted me to use, has not fully obeyed me for many years, and has been rebelling in her heart about some things I have dealt with her to change. You look on the outward appearance, while I look at the heart." Of course, brother Hagin learned a valuable lesson that day, and one that we all must strive to remember when we are ready to pick up stones.

Russell Plilar, a very close friend of mine and Pastor of Seedtime and Harvest Church in San Diego, said, "The devil is not concerned about your past. It's your future he's interested in." He went on to say, "If the enemy thinks enough of our future to fight against it, we should think enough of our future to fight for it." He added, "The devil is not concerned about losers, he is after winners." One of Pastor Russell's favorite quotes is, "Your future is bright—but it will require a fight." Of course, he is speaking of the fight of faith (1 Timothy 6:12).

Sometimes your obstacles may include religious or self-righteous people who will try to stand in your way. Moses, Jeremiah, Isaiah, Jesus, Paul, and all most all of God's champions faced hypocrites and self-righteous dream busters. Somehow these self appointed, misguided souls feel their self justification qualifies them to distance themselves from those who have stumbled along the way. This leaves them with a false sense of exclusivity and importance before God. This was true of a dear friend of our family, whom we will call Mary.

Mary had been divorced twice, due to both husbands violating the marriage covenant and not repenting. Finally, after trying to heal the marriage, (in both instances) she took her scriptural grounds for divorce. Of course, the Job comforters came around, and began to accuse, ostracize, and criticize her. Not knowing the whole story, but needing to feel pious, they started the rumor mill that Satan wanted. Even spiritual leaders in nearby churches and ministries were involved in tongue wagging. However, God intervened, and now she is happily married to a man that loves her, cherishes her, and works alongside her in ministry and business supporting the work of God. What's amazing is the fact that she has won more souls to the Lord (as a so-called layperson) than some pastors and leaders. She continually supports effective ministries and charitable works; is involved in prison ministry; functions in the revelatory gifts of the Spirit through visions, dreams, and revelations; and has a dedicated prayer life that has impacted the lives of many individuals.

One of the women she impacted was in prison for felony. After months and months of imparting the Word of God into the life of this inmate, the woman gave her life to Jesus Christ. Now this former convicted felon is out of prison, working in a corporate office handling checks, accounts, and assisting with the overall operations of the business. The last I heard, the woman's daughter was attending a Christian academy and doing quite well. This convert is one of many such testimonies credited to this "wounded" sister's heavenly account.

I thank God this mighty woman of God did not fall victim to the enemy's plan and give up, or faint because someone thought she was a loser or unfit to work in God's vineyard.

As we read on in Luke 18, we find the publican did not even lift up so much as his eyes unto heaven, but smote upon his breast saying, *"God be merciful to me a sinner."* Jesus said that this man (the publican) went down to his house justified, rather than the pious Pharisee.

I think most of us have been like the Pharisee, which is probably why Jesus related this incident. The story serves to remind us that there is none righteous in themselves, and that only by the grace of God and the blood of Jesus Christ can any of us expect to see God in peace. If you notice, it was this same attitude that we read about earlier with the other servants that went out into the field during the early hours of the day. They were angry with the lord of the vineyard because He dealt the same wage to every man, regardless of when he started.

Some people feel they are doing God a great service by participating with His plan. They do not realize it is His mercy that allows Him to use the (perceived) best of His children. Now, I am not implying that holy living is not imperative, but the attitude of our heart is more important than an outward show of piety that we really do not walk in or possess. To become holy like the Lord, we should be merciful like the Lord. Most of us (me included) have a long way to go in this regard. He told the Pharisees, "I will have mercy and not sacrifice." They weighed people down with the letter of the law, but did not know how to lift one finger to help a brother or sister fulfill the law. Please do not take what I am saying here as a lever to rebuke a brother or sister who, under the anointing of God, is exhorting another believer to stop sinning and to overcome through Jesus Christ. There are times we must speak a word of admonishment to a brother or sister, but we must do it in love and with the right motivation, and based upon the Word of God.

God Is a Restorer of Broken Vessels

In the book of Jeremiah we see how God instructed the prophet to go down to a potter's house to watch him work. The potter was busy making a fine pot for sale, no doubt, but suddenly it was marred in the potter's hands.

Often times the clay the potter was working with had flaws that did not show up immediately when he began to form the vessel. However, as the potter continued applying pressure on the clay to form it into the object he wanted, it buckled under and was flawed.

While attending college in Montana, I took a pottery course as an elective. Just through that experience, I came to realize that sometimes after much work on a piece of pottery, it would become flawed and need to be remolded. This is how it is with many of you who are reading this message. You have buckled under the hand of Almighty God. You have seen a gaping hole in your personality that has let all the wind out of your sails. The good news is the story in Jeremiah does not end with a faulty piece of pottery!

Jeremiah kept watching the potter, and possibly to his utter amazement, the potter did not throw the clay away. Let me edify, encourage, and exhort you who feel unworthy, unwanted or rejected right now. The Lord wants you to know that He is not through with you. You are His vessel and He wants to change things around in your life and ministry. He wants to put you back in the fields for service and fruitfulness beyond what you can ask or think. He is not going to make you less than His original plan or design. You are precious to Him. He is the Lord, and He changes not. He is the author and finisher of your faith. Just receive His adjustment, and watch what He will do with you.

Although clay was a fairly common substance, it was very valuable to the potter. He had to go out of his way to find this particular clay and he was not about to toss it out. He had already invested much time in putting the clay through the preliminary processes necessary to mold and shape it into a worthwhile object; an object that would catch the eye of shoppers in the market place; an object of beauty, grace, dependability, and functionality.

So what did he do? He started to massage the clay to remove any air pockets that might have formed during his first attempt to shape a masterpiece. Next, the master potter began to roll out any new lumps (calloused areas of the heart and mind). Afterwards, he began to wet the clay (a fresh anointing of the Holy Spirit and the water of the Word) and to form it into a ball. Then he tenderly placed it back onto the potter's wheel, and gently began to make a NEW vessel (Read Jeremiah 18:1-6).

Glory to God! What a classic example to show us that He is in the restoring business! He is able to take your dust and ashes, and then make you into a vessel beyond your wildest dreams. This time He will make sure you have the tensile strength you previously lacked. So my friend, just yield to Him, because He has not changed His mind. He will make you into a vessel of honor. All you need to do is cooperate and allow the process to start.

You might say, "Well, Brother James, you don't know what I did?"

Remember the word of the Psalmist who wrote:

3. *If thou, LORD, shouldest mark iniquities, O Lord, who shall stand?*

4. *But there is forgiveness with thee, that thou mayest be feared.*

PSALMS 130:3-4

None of us can sound our trumpets of perfection or throw stones of condemnation at anyone. This does not mean we cannot judge the fruit of a spiritual leader, teaching, or situation (Matthew 7:16-20), and rebuke with all long suffering and doctrine (2 Timothy 4:2-4), or restore fallen brethren in a spirit of meekness (Galatians 6:1). All of this, however, must be done with the attitude of meekness and humility, lest we forget that we too are dust and that without the grace and mercy of God, "There go I."

Far too often we learn these lessons the hard way. God has to allow some great difficulty in our lives to bring us to a place of brokenness where we can become more compassionate with our fallen brothers and sisters. No, God may not cause these situations but He does allow them, even as He permitted the Israelites to suffer hunger in the wilderness (not giving them the luxury of enjoying tasty foods).

> *And he humbled thee, and suffered thee to hunger, and fed thee with manna, which thou knewest not, neither did thy fathers know; that he might make thee now that man doth not live by bread only, but by every word that proceedeth out of the mouth of the LORD doth man live.*
>
> DEUTERONOMY 8:3

Friend, go back to the Word of God. Discover that His mercies are new EVERY morning. Know that He puts your sins behind His back and blots out all your transgressions, removing them as far as the east is from the west (Psalm 103:5, Isaiah 43:25, Lamentations 3:22-23). Remember that He came to heal the broken hearted. Learn of Him (Matthew 11:29) and recognize that He is the Good Shepherd (Psalm 23:1) that will give rest unto your weary soul.

That's right, if you are heavy laden, Jesus is beckoning for you to come to Him and receive His rest. His arms are open wide, just like the prodigal son's father (Luke 15:11-32).

If you are going to be an end-time servant of Christ you must shake off the past with its trials, failures, and disappointments. You must not insult the Spirit of God, or deny the power of the Blood of Jesus Christ by continuing to look back at the past. You must decide to exalt Jesus Christ and the power of His Blood by taking a firm hold on your prophetic destiny in Him. Walking by faith means we are walking towards what God has promised, and reaching for those things that are in front of us in the Spirit, not looking back at the past. Usually when we are not moving forward, we are either looking back on past glories and successes, or our disappointments and failures.

These truths will never become a reality in us until you open your heart and receive them as the final authority in your life. As long as we keep God and His Word at arm length or try to examine it with a microscope before trusting in it, we will walk in defeat. But if we let the Word of God into our spirit (where it can germinate) it will produce the harvest of faith in that area and change our life completely.

Many people hear the Word of God, but they have built up a wall (inside their mind and soul) that does not allow the Word to penetrate deep enough to take root. The only time the Word of God will have an effect in our lives is when we pull down the strongholds of doubt, fear and unbelief, and embrace the Word of God. You say, "How do we do that, Brother James?" The answer is by taking heed according to God's Word.

Wherewithal shall a young man cleanse his way? by taking heed thereto according to thy word.
PSALM 119:9

Taking heed means paying attention to in order to take action. In other words, you must be willing to admit that you have stopped following God's will completely and receive His cleansing (1 John 1:9). Next, you must take proactive steps to grow in His Word and grace each day and set your mind to serve Him with a pure heart.

Finally, you must put your hand to the plow and not look back. By taking this type of action, you will be cooperating to expedite and help bring about the restoration and healing you need in your soul. God's waiting on you!

The Father is no respecter of persons, however, He does respect faith (Hebrews 11:6) and obedience (Isaiah 1:18-19). If you step out on His Word, and lean upon Him with all your heart, He will not forsake you. Even in the toughest places, you will know His strength and power. He hastens his Word to perform it (Jeremiah 1:12).

There is yet another group of saints that have lived for God faithfully and had little fruit or manifestation of His power in their lives or ministry. I believe the time is here for them to rise up and put a demand on that which belongs to them (not haughtily, but in faith). The Lord wants them to covet earnestly the best gifts and to seek Him for a strategy to reach souls. If we seek—we shall find. That is His promise.

If you fall into this category, you may be saying, "I am waiting on God." I believe He is saying, "I am waiting on you to obey what I have already shown you before I will give you more." You see fear has immobilized some to the point they are afraid to even share their faith with someone across the street or in the grocery store. We know that fear is an enemy of God, for the scripture says,

> *For God hath not given us the spirit of fear; but of*
> *power, and of love, and of a sound mind.*
> 2 TIMOTHY 1:7

The Lord has already given us the keys to the Kingdom and whatever we permit on earth is being permitted in Heaven, but whatever we forbid on earth is already forbidden in Heaven. Let us therefore forbid fear to dominate our thinking and lives. Fear is the opposite of faith and trust, so we must make a conscious decision to cast it out of our thinking and conversation. Then let us daily remember to put on the full armor of God, praying in the Spirit, and being watchful at all times. God is mobilizing a last day army from around the world that is going beyond the norm. And, even though it is the eleventh hour, you can be a part of this vast army of disciplined and anointed soldiers.

Please take this message as an encouragement, and move out in obedience to accomplish all He has called you to do. Ask Him to help you pursue His plan for your life with a fully surrendered heart. The manifestation of your calling, anointing, gifting, and purpose will not be noticeable over night, but it can begin to bud and flourish much sooner than you think. The healing miracles will flow. The financial provision will come. The signs and wonders will be in continual demonstration. This will all be a result of your willing obedience to walk by faith in His word.

I am persuaded to believe you are reading this book because you have a desire to fulfill God's destiny for your life, and realize that time is very short, not only for America, but the world as we know it.

Finding Your Gift and Making It Count for Jesus

I n Matthew's gospel we find the parable of a king who gave his servants talents and called them into account concerning their investment and increase of those talents.

Matthew 25:13-30 reads:

13. *Watch therefore, for ye know neither the day nor the hour wherein the Son of man cometh.*

14. *For the kingdom of heaven is as a man travelling into a far country, who called his own servants, and delivered unto them his goods.*

15. *And unto one he gave five talents, to another two, and to another one; to every man according to his several ability; and straightway took his journey.*

16. *Then he that had received the five talents went and traded with the same, and made them other five talents.*

17. And likewise he that had received two, he also gained other two.

18. But he that had received one went and digged in the earth, and hid his lord's money.

19. After a long time the lord of those servants cometh, and reckoneth with them.

20. And so he that had received five talents came and brought other five talents, saying, Lord, thou deliveredst unto me five talents: behold, I have gained beside them five talents more.

21. His lord said unto him, Well done, thou good and faithful servant: thou hast been faithful over a few things, I will make thee ruler over many things: enter thou into the joy of thy lord.

22. He also that had received two talents came and said, Lord, thou deliveredst unto me two talents: behold, I have gained two other talents beside them.

23. His lord said unto him, Well done, good and faithful servant; thou hast been faithful over a few things, I will make thee ruler over many things: enter thou into the joy of thy lord.

24. Then he which had received the one talent came and said, Lord, I knew thee that thou art an hard man, reaping where thou hast not sown, and gathering where thou hast not strawed:

25. And I was afraid, and went and hid thy talent in the earth: lo, there thou hast that is thine.

26. *His lord answered and said unto him, Thou wicked and slothful servant, thou knewest that I reap where I sowed not, and gather where I have not strawed:*

27. *Thou oughtest therefore to have put my money to the exchangers, and then at my coming I should have received mine own with usury.*

28. *Take therefore the talent from him, and give it unto him which hath ten talents.*

29. *For unto every one that hath shall be given, and he shall have abundance: but from him that hath not shall be taken away even that which he hath.*

30. *And cast ye the unprofitable servant into outer darkness: there shall be weeping and gnashing of teeth.*

The Eleventh Hour Servants realize that the Lord is not just returning to rapture the Church, but is also coming back to reward the faithful.

Revelation 22:12 says:

And, behold, I come quickly; and my reward is with me, to give every man according as his work shall be.

Did you notice how the lord rewarded the man with two talents equally as he did the man with the five talents? The reason is because both servants were industrious and used the talents to increase his kingdom. They did not have the same amount of talents, but he gave them an equal reward based upon what they had been given, and how they handled its use and increase. God may call some to be apostles or prophets or teachers, but they will not be rewarded for their callings, they will be rewarded for their faithfulness and fruitful ministry to Him in the thing(s) He has graced them with. Regardless of your call, just remain faithful, and you will not lose your reward. Focus on doing your part to finish what the Lord has called you to do. Your goal must be to work towards reaching the harvest in the capacity in which He has called you to function, while edifying the Body of Christ.

There are gifts and callings within everyone in the Body of Christ, but not all are responding to the call. Paul said that he was not disobedient to the heavenly vision (Acts 26:19). Therefore, when it was time for him to depart, he could boldly say "I have fought a good fight, I have kept the faith. Henceforth there is laid up for me a crown of righteousness..." (2 Timothy 4:7-8).

Countless people in the Body of Christ are not functioning in their place because they are not plugged into a local church where they can grow, develop, mature, and become fruitful and complete in all that God has called them to do and become. We can compare this to an electric keyboard that has several piano, organ, string, brass, woodwind, bass, percussion, and synthesizer sounds. It may be a very fine, state-of the-art keyboard, but if it is not plugged in, it won't work. God has designed you and me the same way. If we are not plugged into the rest of the Body, we cannot function in the full capacity that He ordained.

The Body of Christ and the Local Church

L ast, but not least, the Eleventh Hour Servants will be men and women who are joined to the rest of the Body of Christ in a practical and meaningful way. In other words, they will not be lone rangers or aloof from other Christians. They will find their place in the Body of Christ and put their shoulder to the work of winning the lost and reaping the harvest.

Often we find individuals that have been wounded in the Church. They leave a local fellowship or congregation vowing they will no longer trust another believer, pastor, or church. These individuals try to make it on their own, and may seem to have some success, but they will never achieve the fullness of what God has for them alone. Just as the head needs the feet, the feet need the head. All of us are to be interdependent members within the Body of Christ.

The Eleventh Hour Servants are learning that the local church or assembly holds the key to their fruitfulness. They have learned that in order to fulfill their destiny they must likewise be vitally connected and involved in helping others in the Body fulfill their God given destinies. Not only will these servants need to be a part of a local church or assembly, they will also need to be involved in body ministry that will enable them to utilize their gifts and callings to build up the other members of Christ.

These end-time servants will be men, women, boys, and girls who have discovered who they are in Christ and what God has enabled them to do. They will not be pew warmers or politically correct in what religious circles demand. Most likely they will be looked upon as odd or not fitting with the others. They may even be considered unruly or unorthodox, but God will anoint and commission them for this last hour, last harvest, and last chance to work in His fields. They will be radical for Jesus Christ, and throw off the self-made restraints of man, but still be submitted within the local assembly according to God's Word. As leaders, we must see these people for what they are, and not hold them back, lest we fight the very end-time prophetic purposes of God, as the scribes and Pharisees did in the beginning of the early Church.

These servants will not be content to sit in church Sunday after Sunday while the world goes to hell. They will not be satisfied with just another juicy teaching or sermonette. Instead, they will want to be involved in winning the lost, preaching the gospel, laying hands upon the sick, casting out demons, and raising the dead, in Jesus' Name.

Within this group of servants some will be like Moses, the man of stammering lips; Isaiah, the man of unclean lips; Jeremiah the one who felt too young to do the work of the Lord; Saul of Tarsus, the persecutor of the Church who fought against the ways of God; and even Peter who denied Christ three times. To the world they may look like a rag tag bunch, but to Jesus, they will be prophetic destiny in action. They will be fulfillment of God's plan for the ages.

I believe these servants will be instrumental in bringing the Church to its full potential. They will be the end-time army of which Joel prophesied—the sons and daughters that will prophesy, the young men that will have visions, and the old men that will dream dreams.

The Eleventh Hour Servants will be those that appreciate and utilize the gifts and callings of God to their fullest potential. They will not be moved by the opinions of men. The Eleventh Hour Servants will move in the Spirit and not give into the fickleness of the world or the smugness of lukewarm, pew sitting critics who will not leave their comfort zones to reach out to a lost and dying world

They may not have seminary training or degrees from recognized bible institutes, but they are destined to do great and mighty exploits in the Name of the Lord. God's end-time servants will demonstrate to this generation the message of salvation with signs following.

An Appeal to Church Leadership

Years ago God used me to establish a church, in which I served as senior pastor for several years before turning it over to a young Bible School graduate. Since that time I have functioned on more than one occasion as a staff or associate pastor, traveled and ministered internationally, and for a short time served as Acting Superintendent for a group of nearly thirty churches.

During my tenure as senior pastor, I had the privilege of teaching the congregation about their purpose and role in the church, and their gifts and callings. It was not totally unusual for me to sit down on a Sunday morning or Wednesday night and give the service over to one of my staff leadership. I knew they would never have the ability to impact the world, if they never had the chance to impact the local assembly. I realized that as a Five-fold ministry gift, I was ordained to feed the sheep, but also to equip and train the sheep. God convicted me early in my ministry that others had something from Him as well, and that for the Body to be healthy each joint needed to supply what God had given it to share with the rest of the Body. I realized that as the local head of the church, I did not have to do all of the speaking. I was made aware that others were sent to help the Body to grow (Ephesians 4:16; Romans 12:6 - 8) and not just support my ministry or ego.

Pastors and leaders, let me encourage you to seek God about actually training members of your local congregation, not just in doctrine, but by arranging a place and time for practice and application. That is why I appreciate the ministry of Charles and Frances Hunter so much. They actually demonstrate their conviction that God wants to use all of the Body of Christ in signs, wonders, and gifts of the Holy Spirit. The same is true with other ministries who have been used of God in training tens of thousands of individuals how to activate the gift of prophecy (1 Corinthians 14:31) and other gifts of the Spirit. They not only teach and preach, but insist that the listeners have an opportunity to develop through activation and exercises in the manifestation of spiritual gifts. This is accomplished through setting time aside in their services. I am convinced that leaders who are not taking this similar approach are not truly preparing their congregations for spiritual warfare and evangelism. Believers do not need information only, but they also need impartation, demonstration, and application—if they are truly going to retain and develop in what they have been taught.

The other day I heard a prophet sharing how God wants to use everyone in the Body of Christ to manifest the gifts. He passionately declared that God wants the manifestation of His glory to be seen through the entire Body and not just a few "great" men or women of God. He went on to say, "God wants the manifestation of the gifts to operate in the supermarket and in places outside the church building, because that is what's going to demonstrate to the world that Jesus is Who He claimed to be, the Son of God."

Soldiers are prepared for battle by intense training (not just lectures); training that affords them ample opportunity to "try out" the teachings and equipment they have received. Would you, as a parent, want your child to go to war without having every possible opportunity for the most advanced and detailed training? Yet, we as leaders are preaching sermon after sermon, year after year, to a great number of people who are basically ignorant of spiritual gifts (1 Corinthians 12:1) and who have never been allowed or given a safe environment to manifest the gifts God has given them (1 Corinthians 12:7; 14:26, 31; 1 Peter 4:10). With this said, I appeal to leaders to prayerfully consider if they are following the true scriptural guidelines for their church services, or simply following the advice of their peers or advisory boards. I realize it may be more comfortable to do the latter, but we are called to equip and mobilize, not baby-sit and fossilize.

Spiritual Conditions in the Church

In writing this chapter, I am aware that not everyone in the Body of Christ is on the same level of maturity, experience, or revelation. On the other hand, there are multitudes of believers with more than ample opportunities to bear fruit for the Kingdom of God, and yet are seeing little or no results due to reasons we will begin to address.

Before dealing with those issues, I would like to say "hats off" to our dear brothers and sisters around the world who are totally dedicated and sold out to God. Those that are "putting their necks to the work" of their Lord (Nehemiah 3:5). Many of these believers have never been to a seminar, traditional church service, Bible college, or seminary, yet are being persecuted for their robust faith and steadfastness in the Lord. They risk their jobs, possessions, and lives to take the gospel to their generation and nation. These men, women, boys, and girls are giants of the faith and deserve our continual prayer, support, and encouragement.

If you will look at the church of Jesus Christ you will see that there is a wide range of believers from "on fire" to "ice cold." There is also an emphasis on various teachings, such as the new

The Eleventh Hour Servants

birth, giving, faith, love, spiritual warfare, spiritual gifts, healing, signs and wonders, ministry gifts, emotional healing, marriage, family life, and more. These are excellent doctrines and topics of which the church should continue to teach and preach, however, unless we move out of head knowledge into a real experiential dimension of power and service for the King, we will be considered as useless salt that has lost its savor, and therefore good for nothing but to be trodden under foot of men. If we look back at history, we see that God allowed His people to be trampled down by their enemies and engulfed with spiritual darkness over and over again, and all because of their refusal to be His "salt and light" in the earth.

Most likely, the persons primarily addressed by this book will be those who are members of Evangelical, Fundamental, Charismatic, and Nondenominational churches. The majority have listened to powerful messages through well-rounded and biblically sound ministry gifts or even attended bible colleges and seminaries. Quite often they show up at crusades and special meetings, and have several Bible translations, study aids, teaching tapes, videos, and books for resources. Yet, they are basically living for themselves or just trying to survive and enjoy the best of this life until Jesus returns. If you questioned many of them, they would admit they have not borne any significant fruit for the Lord of the Harvest, but most of them believe God for a BIG MANSION in the sky-in the sweet by and by.

A number of these individuals have gotten caught up with the cares of life, trying to endure economic pressures, while

52

others have gotten cold, fearful, or bitter through a series of negative events they have experienced in life. Several have fallen into immorality, financial ruin, or other tragedies. Still others have become discouraged, overcome with grief, or dismayed with God due to a seeming unanswered prayer request or the loss of a close friend or loved one.

Some believers know beyond a shadow of any doubt that they have a special calling from God, but inwardly recognize it will cost them to obediently follow the Lord. So instead of surrendering to the call, they choose to stay in their comfort zones. A great number have not esteemed the call of God valuable or worthwhile, and consequently they have lost their fervor for Him and are caught up with the world and the pleasures of this life.

Of course, there are those who are sincere about serving the Lord. They have a prayer life, attend a local fellowship, and are students of the Bible, yet they have gotten caught up in the politics of religion, and are waiting for mans approval and acknowledgment before they step out for Christ. Somehow, they believe they must have a position or recognition in the church before they can successfully go out and do the works of Jesus. They mistakenly feel they must have a special word from a leader of the church to do the exploits God commissioned all His children to do in this hour. Please understand that I wholly believe in prophetic ministers giving special words over individuals to confirm their gifts and callings (1 Timothy 4:14). However, I see nothing in scripture that says we must wait for a special group of church leaders to lay hands on us before we can go out and win souls for Jesus Christ. It is our God given duty.

In spite of this condition in many believers today, I am convinced God is making one final call to awaken that part of the Body of Christ that has become lethargic, complacent, and indifferent, full of languor, and asleep. He is searching for Eleventh Hour Servants that will heed His last call for laborers and will fulfill the Great Commission, becoming a vital part of this final great harvest campaign. Could He be speaking to you?

If you see yourself in any of these conditions, start expecting the Holy Spirit to help you move out of neutral into the power, flow, and impact of God's purpose for your life and ministry. We are the ones that must make the adjustment. God's Word says,

> *If my people, who are called by my name, shall humble themselves, and pray, seek my face and turn from their wicked ways, then I will hear from heaven, and will forgive their sin, and will heal their land.*
>
> (2 CHRONICLES 7:14)

He can heal your spiritual land today, if you will turn to Him and pray.

Jesus told the affluent, but indifferent church at Laodicea to anoint their eyes so they might see, and to put on white raiment that they may be clothed, and to buy gold from Him that had been tried in the fire, that they might be rich. What a rebuke! Yet, He still called them to repentance, so they might escape the severe consequences of their disobedience and useless religious exercises.

It appears that the Lord will (as we would say) go out of His way to find a repentant heart that is open to His mercy and grace. It likewise seems clear that He always has His hand stretched out to the sinner and backslider before the consequences of their sins overcome them. Consider the case with Noah, Sodom and Gomorrah, Nineveh, King Nebuchadnezzar, King Ahab, and many others in the passages of scripture. There is an indisputable revelation in each case that He is a merciful God, Whose compassion runs deep.

Hindrances and Stumbling Blocks

Without being critical, negative or condemning, I want us to take a real look at the way things have been and how they must change, before we can truly expect to experience the manifestation of God's power and glory.

Haven't you noticed that many people routinely attend church services Sunday after Sunday, but never seem to really put their hands to the work of the vineyard? And, too, haven't you observed that in most cases it is because they are extremely comfortable watching their televisions or participating in some other recreational activity?

The spirits of Procrastination and Complacency tell these individuals, "You can wait for awhile longer before you start working with the Lord." Those two imps whisper, "Everything is pretty good right now, no need to upset the apple cart by getting involved with soul winning and discipleship. And besides, if you really start serving the Lord, winning the lost, and all that goes with it, you might not have a life." Dear brother or sister, anyone listening to those lies of the enemy and in that condition, does not have a life (not the kind Jesus wants). Those individuals have become self-serving, unproductive, and lazy.

This may sound strong (hopefully you won't quit reading), but when you are waking someone up from the sleep of death, you cannot play paddy cakes. You must take firm action to get the desired results. Conference speaker Joyce Myers once stated that people will either suffer from the discipline and suffering it takes to make right choices or from the regrets and sorrows that come from making wrong choices. Making the wrong choice may seem like the easy way out, but the consequences can be far reaching.

But God is going to do something in you and me, and we are going to find that the best place to be is with Jesus, winning the lost, ministering His healing power, delivering the oppressed, and helping the work of the Kingdom of God in every way possible.

The Return of Jesus Christ

O ne of the great theological subjects dividing the modern day church has been that of the return of Jesus Christ and the "rapture" or catching away of His people the Church.

In 1969, when I was converted, the message you often heard was that the Lord was coming back soon, and that we could be raptured any minute, day, or hour. This message, of course, has been the hope of all Christians since the day the two angels said:

...Ye men of Galilee, why stand ye gazing up into heaven? this same Jesus, which is taken up from you into heaven, shall so come in like manner as ye have seen him go into heaven.

ACTS 1:11

Jesus Himself said:

In my Father's house are many mansions: if it were not so, I would have told you.
I go to prepare a place for you. And if I go and prepare a place for you, I will come again, and receive you unto

myself; that where I am, there ye may be also.
And whither I go ye know, and the way ye know .

JOHN 14:2-4

Throughout the scriptures from Genesis to Revelation there are numerous prophetic passages regarding the coming of the Lord, and also the day of His wrath.   I believe we are living in that generation that will witness those events. Let me explain why.

In Matthew 24 the disciples asked Jesus when the end would come and what would be the signs of His coming.   Jesus gave them a very straight answer that has only been partially fulfilled. In this discourse, He directed their attention to certain signs that must first come to pass.

Let's read it together.

1. *And Jesus went out, and departed from the temple: and his disciples came to him or to shew him the buildings of the temple.*

2. *And Jesus said unto them, See ye not all these things? verily I say unto you, There shall not be left here one stone upon another, that shall not be thrown down.*

3. *And as he sat upon the mount of Olives, the disciples came unto him privately, saying, Tell us, when shall these things be? and what shall be the sign of thy coming, and of the end of the world?*

4. *And Jesus answered and said unto them, Take heed that no man deceive you.*

5. *For many shall come in my name, saying, I am Christ; and shall deceive many.*

6. *And ye shall hear of wars and rumours of wars: see that ye be not troubled: for all these things must come to pass, but the end is not yet.*

7. *For nation shall rise against nation, and kingdom against kingdom: and there shall be famines, and pestilences, and earthquakes, in divers places.*

8. *All these are the beginning of sorrows.*

9. *Then shall they deliver you up to be afflicted, and shall kill you: and ye shall be hated of all nations for my name's sake.*

10. *And then shall many be offended, and shall betray one another, and shall hate one another.*

11. *And many false prophets shall rise, and shall deceive many.*

12. *And because iniquity shall abound, the love of many shall wax cold.*

13. *But he that shall endure unto the end, the same shall be saved.*

14. *And this gospel of the kingdom shall be preached in all the world for a witness unto all nations; and then shall the end come.*

15. *When ye therefore shall see the abomination of desolation, spoken of by Daniel the prophet, stand in the holy place, (whoso readeth, let him understand:)*

16. *Then let them which be in Judaea flee into the mountains:*

17. *Let him which is on the housetop not come down to take any thing out of his house:*

18. *Neither let him which is in the field return back to take his clothes.*

19. *And woe unto them that are with child, and to them that give suck in those days!*

20. *But pray ye that your flight be not in the winter, neither on the sabbath day:*

21. *For then shall be great tribulation, such as was not since the beginning of the world to this time, no, nor ever shall be.*

22. *And except those days should be shortened, there should no flesh be saved: but for the elect's sake those days shall be shortened.*

23. *Then if any man shall say unto you, Lo, here is Christ, or there; believe it not.*

24. *For there shall arise false Christs, and false prophets, and shall shew great signs and wonders; insomuch that, if it were possible, they shall deceive the very elect.*

25. *Behold, I have told you before.*

26. *Wherefore if they shall say unto you, Behold, he is in the desert; go not forth: behold, he is in the secret chambers; believe it not.*

27. *For as the lightning cometh out of the east, and shineth even unto the west; so shall also the coming of the Son of man be.*

28. *For wheresoever the carcass is, there will the eagles be gathered together.*

29. *Immediately after the tribulation of those days shall the sun be darkened, and the moon shall not give her light, and the stars shall fall from heaven, and the powers of the heavens shall be shaken:*

30. *And then shall appear the sign of the Son of man in heaven: and then shall all the tribes of the earth mourn, and they shall see the Son of man coming in the clouds of heaven with power and great glory.*

31. *And he shall send his angels with a great sound of a trumpet, and they shall gather together his elect from the four winds, from one end of heaven to the other.*

32. *Now learn a parable of the fig tree; When his branch is yet tender, and putteth forth leaves, ye know that summer is nigh:*

33. *So likewise ye, when ye shall see all these things, know that it is near, even at the doors.*

34. *Verily I say unto you, This generation shall not pass, till all these things be fulfilled.*

35. *Heaven and earth shall pass away, but my words shall not pass away.*

36. *But of that day and hour knoweth no man, no, not the angels of heaven, but my Father only.*

37. But as the days of Noe were, so shall also the coming of the Son of man be.

38. For as in the days that were before the flood they were eating and drinking, marrying and giving in marriage, until the day that Noe entered into the ark,

39. And knew not until the flood came, and took them all away; so shall also the coming of the Son of man be.

40. Then shall two be in the field; the one shall be taken, and the other left.

41. Two women shall be grinding at the mill; the one shall be taken, and the other left.

42. Watch therefore: for ye know not what hour your Lord doth come.

43. But know this, that if the goodman of the house had known in what watch the thief would come, he would have watched, and would not have suffered his house to be broken up.

44. Therefore be ye also ready: for in such an hour as ye think not the Son of man cometh.

45. Who then is a faithful and wise servant, whom his lord hath made ruler over his household, to give them meat in due season?

46. Blessed is that servant, whom his lord when he cometh shall find so doing.

47. Verily I say unto you, That he shall make him ruler over all his goods.

48. *But and if that evil servant shall say in his heart, My lord delayeth his coming;*

49. *And shall begin to smite his fellowservants, and to eat and drink with the drunken;*

50. *The lord of that servant shall come in a day when he looketh not for him, and in an hour that he is not aware of,*

51. *And shall cut him asunder, and appoint him his portion with the hypocrites: there shall be weeping and gnashing of teeth.*

MATTHEW 24:1-51

Many Bible prophecy teachers have used this passage of scripture as a golden text for the end-times. It has all the components necessary to give a brief, but well-defined explanation of the things that happened shortly (within a few decades) after the resurrection and ascension of our Lord Jesus Christ, but also included events that are yet to take place.

Numerous scholars agree that this passage in Matthew's gospel has a twofold meaning. That is, much of it was to have an immediate fulfillment during the age in which the disciples lived, and the other would encompass the time of the end. Without exaggeration, or any stretch of the imagination, it is clear that this prophecy could have a twofold interpretation, or at least be divided into two or more segments that extended from Jesus' day until the end of the age. How often do we say something that has a twofold application? Why could not God Almighty,

Who is infinite in wisdom and knowledge, do the same? However, without getting too deep into eschatological debate, I would like to present what I believe the scripture plainly warns.

First, Jesus said, "Let no man deceive you." Without question, one of the greatest tests of our day will be staying free from deception, not only by false prophets, but also false brethren. There will even be entities which have supposedly been set up to benefit the government and society that will prove to be totally deceitful in their purpose and goals. Obviously, we are seeing a lot of this in the political realm of our nation and the nations of the world, which is just the tip of the iceberg. What we see in the political realm is also happening in the spiritual realm. There is a parallel of natural to spiritual matters. Dr. Morris Cerullo, founder and president of Morris Cerullo World Evangelism, has stated time and time again, "All truth is parallel." We see many deceitful practices being pawned off as spiritual "truths" and leading many people into deception. New Age philosophies and ideas are creeping into churches and beguiling those who were once grounded in sound doctrine.

Next, Jesus said there would be wars and rumors of wars in various places. Obviously, this has been the state of affairs for centuries, but the companion passage in Luke 21 indicates that it will be worse in the end-times, and that there would be perplexity of nations. Not many would debate that we are living in chaotic times. Nations are rising against nation; there are numerous wars and rumors of wars. There are national and global economic tensions, which undermine the peace and well being of the masses. These are but signs of the end-times.

As a matter of fact, since the inception of this writing in 1998, there has been so much national and international turmoil many people are in dread of a future with the possibility of a nuclear holocaust involving Russia, China, or some other nation. There are situations and developments in Taiwan, North Korea, Cuba, Mexico, and the Middle East that have our intelligence agencies alarmed. There is also a great concern over the threat of terrorism, nuclear, chemical, and biological warfare, even in North America (editors note: this chapter and the bulk of this book were written long before September 11, 2001).

I believe Jesus included our generation when he prophesied of wars and rumors of wars, so if we interpret scripture correctly, the worst is yet to happen. However, God will have a people that will overcome, no matter what happens in the world (Daniel 11:32). He will have an army of saints that will, if need be, lay down their lives for the brethren and the sake of the gospel. These people will not compromise with the pressure of the world nor deny their faith in our risen Savior and soon coming King, Jesus Christ, but be strong and do exploits.

One of the next major points in the Olivet discourse is the mention of famines and pestilence in various locations. Both of these horrible conditions are on the rise. Millions are starving in Africa, Asia, or other parts of the world. In addition, there are major concerns regarding new diseases and biological warfare that could release untold toxic devastation on our society and cause a widespread epidemic of unimaginable proportions. Currently much research is going on around the world, both in antidotes and actual chemical and biological weaponry.

It is not hard to realize how a terrorist or group of terrorists could cause substantial damage to a major metropolitan area in a matter of moments. During some research in 1998, I came across several concerns by our intelligence regarding different possible terrorist attacks. For example, a terrorist in New York could drop a vial of highly lethal chemicals or biological germs in a subway where millions of people travel each day. As the subway trains rush through the subway tunnels in this relatively closed off environment, it would not be long before tens of thousands of these individuals would be infected and spread the deadly disease, causing countless numbers of deaths. Hospitals would be full of urgent care victims and turmoil would run rampant. This sudden outbreak of unprecedented disease and death would be something America or its Western allies have never seen. Such is the world in which we live.

As far as famine is concerned, there have been and will continue to be severe famines that will effect much of the world—even the developed nations that currently know nothing about hunger and lack. In recent years there have been reports that America's food surplus is probably lower than it has been in the last thirty years. Yet, the average American continues to live in a state of ignorance or denial that hunger or famine could ever ravish this land or the developing nations of the world from whom we receive many of our exports.

The handwriting is on the wall, and we will do well to heed the warning. It does not take a rocket scientist to see these things on the horizon. Hopefully, the church of Jesus Christ, in America and the West, will not continue to live in denial and apathy concerning the season in which we are living.

You may be saying, "Brother James, this scares me. I don't want to deal with this right now." Well, obviously these things don't seem pleasant, but Jesus said they would come to pass. The scripture also tells us that *God did not give us the spirit of fear but of power, and of love, and of a sound mind* (2 Timothy 1:7). God does not give us prophetic revelation and insight to scare us, but to prepare us. Even so, a lot of people are talking about the rapture and getting out of here before things get worse.

Certainly, no one probably wants to "escape" these things more than me, but Jesus did not consult with me before He said,

> *"But he that shall endure unto the end, the same shall be saved..."*
>
> MATTHEW 24:13

Obviously, Jesus knew the generation of believers He was speaking about would have to endure some great suffering. Even now, millions of our brothers and sisters in other nations are waiting for the rapture just like we are, but while they are waiting they are enduring some of the greatest persecution the church has ever faced. Reports continue to flood international missionary offices and organizations about believers that have given their lives for the sake of the gospel and the Name of our Lord Jesus. Are we promised that we will escape similar suffering, just because we live in America or the West?

You say, brother James, I thought we were saved by grace, and kept by grace, and therefore should not have to suffer these things! True we are saved by grace, but we still have a responsibility with God's grace (Romans 6:1-2), and His grace does not guarantee we will not face opposition or hard times for our faith (see 1 Peter 1:6-7; 4:1). In the midst of all of this, God's promises give us the confidence that we can do all things through Christ, which strengthens us (Philippians 4:13).

I believe it will be God's grace alone that gives us the ability to stand for Him in these last days and to proclaim His Word to this needy generation. Living for God and being His servants in this hour may require us to suffer persecutions or things we have never dreamed we would face. However, God's Word promises that during the time of great trouble in the world, the righteous shall know their God and do mighty exploits (Daniel 11:32).

God wants fruit for His investment in our lives. We are not robots without wills. We must choose to follow the Lord each day and walk with Him in holiness and Godly fear (Hebrews 12:25-29) regardless of the price. This is not easy or something we can randomly agree to do. The early disciples had to stand against seemingly insurmountable difficulties in order to live for God, and they were severely persecuted for making the choice to follow the Lord and to preach His gospel. Being able to do that took the grace of God. However, if they would have sat down and not released that grace through teaching and preaching (with the accompanying miracles, signs, and wonders), the world would not have been impacted for Jesus. This is clearly evidenced by the Word of God.

Jesus spoke of earthquakes in different places. We have had much earthquake devastation, but the threat of this natural disaster will yet worsen. Although there have been major earthquakes throughout the history of the planet, it seems apparent that Jesus was warning of it becoming increasingly more severe as the day of the Lord draws nearer. Not long before the first draft of this book, a series of major quakes rocked the country of Turkey, killing more than 17,000 people. The earthquakes started in August 1998 and continued several months, causing catastrophic destruction and misery.

While earthquakes were happening in Turkey, there were other earthquakes in Greece, Taiwan, and even a considerable one (with no major damages) here in California. This all happened within three or four months.

The other day, I checked the USGS (U.S. Geological Survey) web-site to see how many earthquakes had taken place within a week or less. It showed that during a period of just four days, there had been twenty-one shocks ranging from 2.8 to 7.4 on the Richter scale, not to mention the scores of smaller shakers. Here in California, it is not unusual to be awakened by tremors or to feel the sudden thud, shaking, or rolling sensation of an earthquake, which is usually accompanied by creaking and cracking sounds throughout houses and buildings.

On October 17, 1989 I was living in the Pasadena area when the Loma Prieta earthquake hit. Houses and buildings shook and shook, for nearly twenty seconds. It was probably one of the most violent earthquakes I had been in, and one that received national attention, even from the White House. Damage and business interruption estimates reached as high as $10 billion, with direct damage estimated at $6.8 billion. President Bush declared a disaster area for the seven hardest-hit counties, from Monterey and San Benito in the south to Marin and Solano in the north.

More than 62 people died, although this was a remarkably low number given the time and size of the earthquake. At least 3,700 people were reported injured and more than 12,000 were displaced. Over 18,000 homes were damaged and 963 were destroyed. Over 2,500 other buildings were damaged and 147 were destroyed.

Right now seismologists are concerned for this same area near San Francisco. They are saying that region is over due for a major quake from the tremendous amount of pressure that is building up along its major fault lines. When this major quake rocks the Bay area, the damages and loss of life could be extensive, especially if the quake has a magnitude of 7.0 or greater like the one that occurred in 1989.

Earthquakes are mentioned in scripture several times, and somehow they seem to parallel events that take place in the spiritual realm. If you look at various passages in the Bible, you will see that earthquakes and major spiritual happenings were often taking place simultaneously. For example, in the book of Amos, we are told that the prophet received the Word of the Lord two years before the earthquake (Amos 1:1). At the crucifixion of Jesus Christ there was an earthquake that caused the centurion and those that were with him to fear greatly and say, *"Truly this was the son of God"* (Matthew 27:54). When our Lord broke the power of death and rose triumphantly from the grave, the angel of the Lord rolled the stone away from the entrance of the tomb causing a great earthquake (Matthew 28:2). *When Paul and Silas were praying and singing praises in prison, suddenly there was a great earthquake* (Acts 16:26). *When the early church prayed there was a great shaking* (Acts 4:31). Over and over we see simultaneous events taking place when earthquakes are spoken of in the scripture. There seems to be evidence that major spiritual happenings are often echoed or preceded by earthquakes. This was the case in 1906 during the great earthquake of San Francisco. The Welsh revival and the Azusa Street outpouring were taking place around that time, as the world was being shaken in both realms. God promised to shake the heavens and the earth during the end-times, just prior to sending His Son (Matthew 24:7; Revelations 6:12; 8:5; 11:13; 16:18; Hebrews 12:26-27). Not only did Jesus say there would be earthquakes, but in the parallel text found in Luke, he mentioned the seas roaring and men's hearts failing for fear of the things that were coming on the earth.

Few people realize that our planet scarcely missed being hit by an asteroid just a few years past. Scientist previously mocked at such a thing happening, but stopped laughing when an asteroid or other heavenly body was recently observed hitting the planet Jupiter. They stated the damage would have been global had it hit the earth. Those types of scenarios would definitely cause men's hearts to fail and become afraid.

Tsunami waves have devastated the Islands of Papua New Guinea within the past few years, and effects from El Nino and La Nina have meteorologists in major concern about the rapidly changing weather patterns. Who ever expected a massive tornado to rush through Salt Lake City, Utah during a "normal" and "peaceful" summer day, wreaking havoc and destruction? Who would have guessed the East Coast would have been hit time after time from hurricane force winds and flooding rains that have left thousands homeless and destitute? Did anyone guess that a major cyclone would whip through India and wipe out an entire community, leaving tens of thousands homeless and over 9,000 dead?

This past decade has set records in major destruction in America, with costs running into the billions. If we are not living in the end-times now, it will be totally unimaginable when it arrives.

Volumes could be written about the concerns scientists have regarding volcanic eruptions in North America along the Cascade mountain range and other locations; or the fear of global warming and glacier melting that could cause major destruction and loss of lives; or the concern over the dangers of nuclear waste and contamination; the loss of crops, reduction in farm production, and food shortages; stock market jitters, mergers, and splits.   Not to mention the concerns among many leaders regarding foreign policies, peace talks, terrorism, global economics, civil violence, and unrest.

Furthermore, there is yet growing uneasiness about computer glitches, computer hackers, and the loss of privacy and human rights for citizens in nearly all countries.   Mixed with all of that is an apprehension over the rising energy costs, the unstable economic roller coaster, racial tensions, Russian and Chinese joint military exercises, national security breaches and espionage, and the continual threat of nuclear and biological warfare.   There is growing distress over the AIDS crisis that is spreading the globe and the rise of other terminal diseases.   Top this off with increased unemployment, teenage pregnancy, crime, violence, and an unending list of other maladies that perplex the most educated minds of our day.

Scientists are progressively experimenting with chip implants to identify animals and humans.   Some researchers have become more and more engrossed with cloning animals, and humans, and someday hope to build a platform that will launch a "super human race."   This of course is leading us right up to the "man of sin."   Never in history has there ever been such near fulfillment of all the things of which Jesus spoke, as with this generation.   By Jesus' standards, we must be living in the last days

The Eleventh Hour Servants

Many people say, "Hey brother, I don't want to hear about troubles. I've got enough of my own." Clearly, that is usually our problem; focusing on our troubles and difficulties, rather than reaching out to help someone else who needs to hear the gospel of Jesus Christ. When God's servant Job got involved with the needs of his friends, by praying for their deliverance, God turned his captivity and blessed him doubly (Job 42:10). I am convinced that God wants to do the same for all of His children that are denying themselves to reach out to the lost and needy.

More and more we have become a generation of victims and wounded people that need constant attention in order to keep going. We have become a generation of high maintenance, low impact Christians that have spent more on counseling, weight loss, cosmetics, entertainment, and fix it programs than we have getting the gospel out. Please don't misunderstand; I believe good biblical counsel can be advantages, especially through a godly pastor, man, or woman of God. But, when we need constant counseling for the same things, with no apparent improvement, and fail to do our part in the healing process, we are wasting our time and money. We fool ourselves by going through this type of activity while expecting a professional counselor to make life better for us.

Of course, we don't want to hear about the troubles ahead, but wouldn't you agree that it's better to know a storm is coming. Such was the case with Noah. He was warned of God and took appropriate action.

By faith Noah, being warned of God of things not seen as yet, moved with fear, prepared an ark to the saving of his house; by the which he condemned the world, and became heir of the righteousness which is by faith.

HEBREWS 11:7

God is sending apostles and prophets throughout the land, many who are not considered great or well known, yet they have an anointed message of power and truth to deliver to today's Church. It is a message of urgency and alarm for those that are dozing in apathy and complacency. It is a message and clarion call of the Spirit of God, saying "Arise Church, and go into the vineyard!" "Put off your slumber and awake unto righteousness and sin not!" "Put your hand to the plow and don't look back!" "The end draws near!"

No, this message that is going across the land is not the tactics of some alarmists that have nothing better to do than frighten cozy, comfortable believers. *This is a message through inspired servants and handmaids of God who have been given a divine mission to awaken those that are at ease in Zion* (Amos 6:1a). My purpose in this writing is to motivate and provoke us to consider the period in which we are living. Time is running out, and there is still much to be accomplished throughout the world—in Jesus' Name. I believe we are the generation that will see the work completed and witness the coming of the Lord.

Twelve

Choosing to Build on the Rock

Here in Southern California there are rainy seasons in which there are major mudslides. During these mudslides it is not unusual for several homes to be destroyed due to their foundations being washed away. Once the foundation is weakened or moved, the house is no longer able to stand. It finally slides down the precipice it was built on, and thus causes the ruin of the house to be substantially great.

In 1998 major news broadcasts showed scenes where several homes along the coast were actually being washed down the slopes they were built upon. It was rather bizarre! These homes were creaking and cracking as they plunged down the side of the cliffs where they once proudly sat. Sadly, though, many were not fully covered with appropriate insurance, which left the owners in financial ruins.

This, of course, is a classic example of what Jesus said about the two men, who built houses. He was paralleling the construction of their houses to adherence and obedience to His Word.

Whosoever cometh to me, and heareth my sayings, and doeth them, I will shew you to whom he is like:

> He is like a man which built an house, and digged deep, and laid the foundation on a rock: and when the flood arose, the stream beat vehemently upon that house, and could not shake it: for it was founded upon a rock. But he that heareth, and doeth not, is like a man that without a foundation built an house upon the earth; against which the stream did beat vehemently, and immediately it fell; and the ruin of that house was great.
>
> LUKE 6:47-49

To stand in this present evil world we must be doers of the Word in an ever increasing manner. We must take a serious look at the inconsistencies we find in our lives, repent, and commit to completely obey the sayings of Jesus. The church of Jesus Christ must wake up and finish the job He has commissioned us to do, and we must do it quickly. Jesus said, *"I must work the works of Him who sent Me, as long as it is day; night is coming, when no man can work"* (John 9:4 NAS; emphasis added).

Note: There is coming an hour in the not too distant future, when we will not enjoy the freedoms we still hold dear. It will be more and more difficult and challenging to preach the gospel, even in America. The devil is not going to sit by and watch as we win the world to Christ. Things will be as they were in the early church: genuine unity of the saints, powerful demonstrations of the Holy Spirit, and severe persecution of believers. Yes, persecution, even in North America.

Thirteen

Demonstrating the Good News

There is a cry in the heart of billions of people around the world for the truth that we often take for granted. We have the goods and the answer for their pain and sinful condition. Therefore we must learn to become fishers of men and reach the unreached with the message of salvation and regeneration through Jesus Christ.

Jesus said follow me, and I will make you fishers of men (Matthew 4:19). That means we will have to walk after His ways, study what He is doing, and how He does things, if we are to be effective soul winners. This will only come through spending time with Him in prayer, study of His Word, meditation on His goodness and promises, and fellowshipping with others who have the same zeal to win the lost. We also should make it a priority to be around ministries that have a heart for the lost and hurting. Seeing God move through these ministries will have a positive effect on our spirits and cause us to grow dramatically. Many times Benny Hinn has credited the late Kathryn Kulhman as the one having the greatest impact on his life. Her constant dependence upon the Holy Spirit and her utter abandonment to Him rubbed off onto Benny, and his life has never been the same. He has impacted millions, but he was first shown the way through her example. We as leaders must be examples to the flock, not just instructors. We must take them into practical training by way of teaching and example. Our pastor often says, "It's better caught than taught."

Maybe you are saying, "I would like to preach the Word or minister the gospel, but I do not know where to begin." Well, obviously you are not going to start preaching Sunday morning at your local church. God does not need everyone in the Body preaching on Sunday morning (this is different than prophecy or spiritual gifts operating in the congregation). He desires everyone in the Body to be actively preaching on Monday through Saturday. When this happens, we can expect the church to be filled on Sunday. This kind of ministry takes place during a break at your job, at the grocery store, the bank, the hospital, the prison or jail, the convalescent home, the juvenile detention center, the athletic club, the restaurant, the high school soccer game, and any other place you might be during the week.

For years now, I have been involved in preaching the Word to prisoners in a federal prison here in San Diego. During that time, we (as a team) have seen over 850 men come forward to receive Christ. Many are transferred to other prisons, but we have received letters from some who tell us how these chapel services have impacted their lives. The chapel where the service is conducted holds less than seventy men, so we are grateful for the number of men that have come to the meetings, heard the gospel, and received eternal life. The other night, the men were not able to meet in the chapel, so the Chaplain took me to one of the floors where nearly 200 inmates are housed. In the center of the floor, there is a recreation area approximately forty-five feet square. After some time, with a seeming uncertain beginning, God came upon me powerfully and allowed me to preach to more than fifty men. At the end of the message, I asked the men to accept Jesus without being ashamed of what others thought. At least thirty-six men came forward, lifted their hands, and prayed out loud to accept the Lord.

All this took place while on lookers were standing by or in their open cell areas around the perimeter of the recreation area. For this to happen, I had to be willing to leave my comfort zone. It would not have happened if I stayed home to watch "Gun Smoke" or some TV special. I had to be willing to go. God did not make me do it. In fact, when I found out we could not have service in the Chapel, my natural inclination was to go home and call it quits for the night, but God had other plans. Hallelujah! Maybe you are not in a situation where you can be a part of a jail or prison ministry outreach. There are still many other possibilities for you to reach the lost.

There have been times where the Lord has privileged me to win someone at a service station pump right after filling my car with gas or at a grocery store. I asked have them to accept the Lord right there. When I was leaving a popular health food store sometime ago, I passed by a set of water machines where people come to refill their water bottles. Suddenly, I noticed an elderly man getting change out to fill his water bottles. Immediately, I was in the spirit, and realized this man had an illness in his body, and had an urge to reach out to him (a word of knowledge, and the compassion of the Lord). I prayed, "Okay Lord, but please help me to have favor with this man and open the door." I went back to the water machines and started talking with the man, and before you knew it, we were discussing health issues and spiritual matters. He confirmed his health issue, and what he was trying to do to cure the situation. I shared with him the gospel, and asked if he would pray with me. He agreed, and I was able to pray with him to receive Jesus Christ, and minister a word for his healing. He was nearly 80 years old and who knows how long he had left to live on this planet, but I was privileged to share Jesus Christ with him and lead him in a prayer of repentance and acceptance of Jesus as Lord. Of course, I am not always able to follow up on all the people that I have led to Christ, but I trust the Father to send more laborers into the path of these new believers to see that they mature and are grounded.

Jesus had a special ability to turn any conversation around to get a word in about the Kingdom of God. A great example is found in the fourth chapter of John's gospel. I encourage you to read it and prayerfully seek the Lord on how you too can share His message with hurting humanity, with signs and wonders following. As you are faithful to share the gospel, you will grow in your witness for Christ and your ability to be sensitive to what and what not to say. The main thing you will be aware of is that most people are starving for love, and if you can show them the love of God, they will listen to you. One point I want to stress here is that you and I cannot determine if we are the ones sowing, watering, or reaping. That is up to the Lord. However, we must seek Him to be sensitive and involved at whatever level of the process He deems necessary.

Fourteen

The Power of the Holy Spirit

God's greatest gift to mankind is Jesus. The greatest gift Jesus has given the Church is the Holy Spirit. Through the Holy Spirit, all the other blessings and manifestations of the Godhead are possible. The Holy Spirit is the giver of wonderful gifts and abilities. In 1 Corinthians 12 and 14, Paul tells us that the Holy Spirit is responsible for manifesting His abilities and wisdom through each believer (1 Corinthians 12:7; 14:26). Yet in most churches, you would not think the Holy Spirit was very generous or giving, because there are not many evidences of His Presence, power, or ministry. This will change in the "eleventh hour." We are going to see mighty demonstrations of the Holy Spirit through the Church of Jesus Christ that will testify of Jesus and the goodness of God Almighty.

The Eleventh Hour Servants will be vitally connected, guided and empowered by the Holy Spirit. They will not follow the formalities of tradition and religion, but have a vital relationship with the Third Person of the Godhead, the Holy Spirit. They will know what *"the communion of the Holy Ghost"* is which Paul mentioned in 2 Corinthians 13:14. They will know what Jesus was speaking about when He said,

The Eleventh Hour Servants

"...but ye shall receive power, after that the Holy Ghost is come upon you..."

ACTS 1:8

Through the vivid night vision the Lord gave me years ago, revealing the massive end-time wave of His power that is coming, I am convinced that the Eleventh Hour Servants will know what it is to be motivated, empowered, controlled and led by the Holy Spirit. They will know that the work being done through them is not by might, nor by power, but by the Spirit of God (Zechariah 4:6). You and I will have to know the Holy Spirit more than anyone else on the planet. We will have to make knowing and following Him a passion and continual quest.

Jesus said out of our innermost being rivers of living water would flow. This, of course, is talking about the Holy Spirit (John 7:37-39). Let's begin to cultivate a deeper relationship with the Holy Spirit. Let's begin to allow Him to be in charge of our praying, preaching, witnessing, and ministry. Let's begin to surrender our wills and lives to Him in an unprecedented manner. Agreed, this is not easy at first, but it will become addictive once you do. You will realize that nothing good can come out of your independent efforts or polished talents, and that only through the power of the Holy Spirit can any of us truly accomplish the will of God.

Conclusion

I have often wondered why the Lord would reward those who obey His Word and win the lost. After all, "It's not by might nor by power, but by the Spirit of God." Why and how can God be justified in rewarding us, when we can do nothing without Him anyway? Finally, I saw one aspect that I believe is a major factor. It is not that we are accomplishing miracles or great works in our own strength or name that brings a reward. It is the fact that we are obeying and cooperating with Lord. Our obedience, and the fruit of it, is what He calls work. It is from this aspect, I believe, that He desires to reward us.

Let's face it, obedience is work! It is not easy to deny oneself, face persecution and misunderstanding, walk in forgiveness, bring the body under submission to the Lord's will, fast, and pray. Yes, it is all by His grace, but there is still a price we must pay in following God's Word and an effort we must exert to cooperate with the grace He so freely gives us (1 Corinthians 15:10). Remember the command of Moses, *"You shall serve the Lord with all your heart, strength, and might."* That's work, and that is one reason the Lord will reward us in that day. The scripture says that He is coming to reward us for our works-good or bad.

My prayer is that the Lord has used this brief writing to exhort and encourage you to go into His vineyard. Jesus is coming soon with crowns and rewards for those that are faithfully fulfilling their part in this end-time harvest of souls.

The Eleventh Hour Servants

Arise, shine; for thy light is come, and the glory of the LORD is risen upon thee. For, behold, the darkness shall cover the earth, and gross darkness the people: but the LORD shall arise upon thee, and his glory shall be seen upon thee. (Isaiah 60:1-2) That time and season is upon us. What a great time to be living, and an awesome time to be an integral part of the Kingdom of God! Make your commitment today to become one of His Eleventh Hour Servants!

To contact James for books, or to schedule him to speak at your church, write or call:

James Brown
Word Of Grace International Ministries
C/O 8555 Aero Dr. Ste. 300
San Diego, CA 92123
623-764-6017